Lucy Larcom

Childhood Songs

Lucy Larcom

Childhood Songs

ISBN/EAN: 9783741123184

Manufactured in Europe, USA, Canada, Australia, Japa

Cover: Foto ©Lupo / pixelio.de

Manufactured and distributed by brebook publishing software (www.brebook.com)

Lucy Larcom

Childhood Songs

BY

LUCY LARCOM.

Illustrated.

BOSTON:
JAMES R. OSGOOD AND COMPANY,
LATE TICKNOR & FIELDS, AND FIELDS, OSGOOD, & CO.
1875.

Entered according to Act of Congress, in the year 1874,
BY JAMES R. OSGOOD & CO.,
in the Office of the Librarian of Congress, at Washington.

UNIVERSITY PRESS: WELCH, BIGELOW, & CO.,
CAMBRIDGE

TO

PRINCE HAL AND LITTLE QUEEN MAUDE

This Book is Dedicated

BY THEIR

LOYAL AND LOVING FRIEND.

NOTE.

IN naming these little poems "Childhood Songs," one especial thought was that not all of them were written from the child's point of view, but as one may write who in mature life retains a warm sympathy with childhood, through a vivid memory of her own. Many of them have already been published, the larger proportion in "Our Young Folks," and two or three in a previous volume; but quite a number are new, having been prepared expressly for this book.

If little children, and those who love little children, find pleasure in these songs, their author will feel it a real happiness to have written them.

L. L.

I bring you these little song-blossoms;
   They grew in my working-field:
No wonderful beauty or splendor
   Can a trodden footpath yield:

But the breezes of childish laughter,
   And the light in a baby's eye,
To the homeliest road bring a freshness
   As free as the blue of the sky.

And I, for one, would much rather,
   Could I merit so sweet a thing,
Be the poet of little children
   Than the laureate of a king.

CONTENTS.

	PAGE
IN TIME'S SWING	19
NEW-YEAR SONG	23
PRINCE HAL	25
AT QUEEN MAUDE'S BANQUET	29
PEEPSY	31
IN THE TREE-TOP	40
BABY'S DAY	42
THE BABY'S THOUGHTS	47
MOONSHINE	50
HAL'S BIRTHDAY	53
A HAREBELL	57
SIR ROBIN	59
GOWNS OF GOSSAMER	62
CALLING THE VIOLET	66
THE RIVULET	70
THE BROWN THRUSH	72
SPRING WHISTLES	74
PLAYTHINGS	79
GIPSY CHILDREN'S SONG	82
MANITOU'S GARDEN	85
DUMPY DUCKY	89
PUSSY-CLOVER	94
BERRYING SONG	97

CONTENTS.

SWINGING ON A BIRCH-TREE	101
LITTLE NANNIE	104
A LILY'S WORD	106
RED SANDWORT	108
GRACE'S FRIENDS	111
THE BROOK THAT RAN INTO THE SEA	116
THE LAST FLOWER OF THE YEAR	119
JESSIE'S BOOK	121
RED-TOP AND TIMOTHY	124
FLOWER-GIRLS	127
THE CLOCK-TINKER	130
CAT-QUESTIONS	132
A FACE IN THE TONGS	135
THE BARN WINDOW	137
A LITTLE CAVALIER	143
IN FAIRY LAND	149
SISTER AND BLUEBIRDS	152
FARTHER ON	155
SWING AWAY	159
THE ROADSIDE PREACHER	161
WHAT THE TRAIN RUN OVER	165
STARLIGHT	171
IF I WERE A SUNBEAM	173
BRING BACK MY FLOWERS	175
SNOW SONG	177
NEW-YEAR'S WISHES	179
ON THE STAIRWAY	183
THE LITTLE TAMBOURINE GIRL	186
AT NIGHTFALL	189
CHRISTMAS GREEN	194
MY CHILDREN	199

LIST OF ILLUSTRATIONS.

	PAGE
PRINCE HAL	*Frontispiece*
IN TIME'S SWING	18, 20
NEW-YEAR SONG	23
PEEPSEY	33
IN THE TREE-TOP	40
BABY'S DAY	42–45
MOONSHINE	50
HAL'S BIRTHDAY	54
THE HAREBELL	57
SIR ROBIN	59
CALLING THE VIOLET	66
THE RIVULET	70
THE BROWN THRUSH	72
SPRING WHISTLES	75
GIPSY CHILDREN'S SONG	82
MANITOU'S GARDEN	85
DUMPY DUCKY	91
BERRYING SONG	97
SWINGING ON A BIRCH-TREE	100
A LILY'S WORD	106
RED SANDWORT	108
GRACE'S FRIENDS	111
THE BROOK THAT RAN INTO THE SEA	116

THE LAST FLOWER OF THE YEAR	119
JESSIE'S BOOK	121
RED-TOP AND TIMOTHY	124
FLOWER-GIRLS	127, 128
CAT-QUESTIONS	133
THE BARN-WINDOW	137, 139
A LITTLE CAVALIER	143
FARTHER ON	155
SWING AWAY	159
STARLIGHT	170
SNOW SONG	177
NEW-YEAR'S WISHES	179
AT NIGHTFALL	191, 193
CHRISTMAS GREEN	194, 197

CHILDHOOD SONGS.

CHILDHOOD SONGS.

IN TIME'S SWING.

FATHER TIME, your footsteps go
Lightly as the falling snow.
In your swing I'm sitting, see!
Push me softly; one, two, three,
Twelve times only. Like a sheet
Spreads the snow beneath my feet.
Singing merrily, let me swing
Out of winter into spring.

Swing me out, and swing me in!
Trees are bare, but birds begin
Twittering to the peeping leaves
On the bough beneath the eaves.

Look! one lilac-bud I saw!
Icy hillsides feel the thaw.
April chased off March to-day;
Now I catch a glimpse of May.

O the smell of sprouting grass!
In a blur the violets pass,
Whispering from the wild-wood come
Mayflowers' breath, and insects' hum.
Roses carpeting the ground;
Orioles warbling all around.
Swing me low, and swing me high,
To the warm clouds of July!

Slower now, for at my side
White pond-lilies open wide.

IN TIME'S SWING.

Underneath the pine's tall spire
Cardinal-blossoms burn like fire.
They are gone; the golden-rod
Flashes from the dark green sod.
Crickets in the grass I hear;
Asters light the fading year.

Slower still! October weaves
Rainbows of the forest-leaves.
Gentians fringed, like eyes of blue,
Glimmer out of sleety dew.
Winds through withered sedges hiss:
Meadow-green I sadly miss.
O, 't is snowing; swing me fast,
While December shivers past!

Frosty-bearded Father Time,
Stop your footfall on the rime!
Hard your push, your hand is rough;
You have swung me long enough.

"Nay, no stopping," say you? Well,
Some of your best stories tell,
While you swing me — gently, do! —
From the Old Year to the New.

NEW-YEAR SONG.

THERE's a New Year coming, coming
    Out of some beautiful sphere,
  His baby-eyes bright
  With hope and delight:
We welcome you, Happy New Year!

There's an Old Year going, going
    Away in the winter drear;

His beard is like snow,
And his footsteps are slow:
Good by to you, weary Old Year!

The New Year comes smiling, smiling,
While the Old Year hastens away,
Unwilling to be
The one sorrow to see,
In a world so enchanting and gay.

The Old Year goes sighing, sighing;
Once he was a baby Year:
His welcome was glad;
But his farewell is sad;
He has nothing to stay for here.

There is always a New Year coming;
There is always an Old Year to go;
And never a tear
Drops the happy New Year,
As he scatters his gifts on the snow.

PRINCE HAL.

PRINCE HAL is a widow's baby;
   His father he never knew.
In the waning of summer he opened
   His eyes of the ocean's blue.

And his mother with tender trouble
   Gazed into their azure deep,
Whence the cloud of some unknown sorrow
   Seemed, vague as a mist, to creep.

It broke on her heart in winter, —
   A knell from the torrid isles
Where a death-sleep fell on her husband:
   But the babe wore his father's smiles;

And all who beheld him loved him,
  Prince Hal, with the eyes of blue
Under the spirit-like forehead, —
  Pale blossom of light and dew.

What recks Prince Hal of the season,
  Enthroned on his mother's arm?
Thick snow through the air is falling,
  But baby and bud are warm.

For buds are the nurslings of tempests,
  And grief may cradle a joy.
On the widow's heart lies a sorrow
  Whose age is the age of her boy.

But he, in the snow-wreath's glimmer,
  Sees nothing but bloom and mirth.
To the royal soul of a baby
  One fairy realm is the earth.

PRINCE HAL.

Prince Hal, he is like his father,
    As a prince resembles a king;
In the crown of a manly nature,
    That is nobler than anything.

For an empty crown is a bauble;
    And he is a sovereign alone,
Who lives to bring joy unto others,
    And to make their trouble his own.

Prince Hal is the son of a widow;
    His father went sailing away
To inherit a far-off kingdom; —
    The boy will follow, some day.

Though his mother her lifelong sorrow
    Measures out by his childish years,
Their length is the span of a rainbow
    That bridges a gulf of tears.

He has cheered us all, as a sunbeam
    Strikes into the heart of a storm;
Through the gladness of little children
    Are the frostiest lives kept warm.

Prince Hal, they alone are true princes
    Who make this old world bloom anew
With the grace and the glory of manhood;
    Great things are expected of you!

AT QUEEN MAUDE'S BANQUET.

SHE wears no crown
    Save her own flossy curls, —
Rosiest, plumpest
    Of pet baby-girls;
Blue-eyed and dimpled
    And dignified she,
Pouring out for us
    Invisible tea, —
        Little Queen Maude.

Tiniest teacup
    And saucer and spoon: —
Baby, your banquet
    Has ended too soon.

Fancy's full cupboard
  Unlocks to your hand;
We, your true subjects,
  Await your command,
    Little Queen Maude.

Throned on the floor,
  We must stoop to your state:
If a queen's little,
  Can courtiers be great?
Now kiss us, dismiss us,
  Red lips rosy-sweet,
For yonder's a poet
  Chained fast to your feet,
    Little Queen Maude.

PEEPSY.

GIRL PEEPSY to the baby sang
   A drowsy little tune;
But all the while the baby lay
   And whimpered for the moon.

"Dear little baby!" Peepsy said,
   "Don't reach your arms out so!
But shut your eyes, and right away
   To fetch the moon I'll go."

"Now breaking promises is bad,—
   As bad as telling lies,"
Said Peepsy, for the babe in sleep
   That instant closed his eyes.

"And I must go and fetch the moon
    Before my brother wakes:
He shall not say that Peepsy-girl
    Her promise ever breaks.

"And there the moon hangs on the hill,
    Our cottage door close by.
I must run fast, or it will slip
    Out into the deep sky."

The cricket chirped, "Quick! Peepsy!—quick!"
    "Quick! quick!" the katydid
Called from the elm-tree by the gate:
    Down from her chair she slid.

She could not reach her broad-brimmed hat;
    Upon the peg it hung.
She shut the cottage door; the gate
    Behind her softly swung.

The rippling brook laughed up at her,
   With all its twinkling eyes;
But rustling leaves to forest-birds
   Were whispering lullabies.

And trees and rocks were fast asleep,
   Folded in shadows black,
As little Peepsy trudged along
   The ferny mountain-track.

The whippoorwills went gossiping
   From silent tree to tree,
Among the gray eavesdropping bats; —
   So strange it was to see

A little girl at nightfall climbed
   The steep and lonesome hill:
But bravely Peepsy hurried on,
   Beneath the starlight still.

A wind came rushing down the rocks,
    And sighed, "Where, Peepsy, where?"
"After the moon!" The light wind laughed,
    And lifted Peepsy's hair.

And kissed her forehead, and went on.
    An owl called, "Who, child, who?"
"My name is Peepsy, if you please!
    May I just pass by you?

"I'm only going to get the moon;
    You're willing, Mr. Owl?"
Poor Peepsy trembled; — such a laugh!
    It sounded like a howl.

And all the forest rang, "Hoo — hoo!
    The like was never heard!"
Ten owls flew down and stared at her;
    But she said not a word.

For now the moon seemed close at hand;
   But oh! she almost cried:
It was too large for her to lift
   Down to the baby's side.

If she could only reach its edge,
   So even and so round,
And send it trundling like a hoop
   Along the mossy ground!

Alas! it was too far! too far!
   Though she on tiptoe stood.
"O pretty stars!" she called aloud,
   "Will you be very good,

And give the moon a push this way?"
   The silly stars, they wink,
But will not budge. She sits her down
   Upon a rock to think,

And wonder why boys ask for things
   Girls cannot get for them: —
But look! the Lady Moon lifts off
   Her crescent-diadem,

And slips the happy Peepsy in!
   See! like a silver sledge
It dashes down the gloomy hill,
   Past glen and gorge and ledge!

It glides along the garden walk,
   It stops beside the door!
Has katydid or cricket seen
   Wonders like this before?

"Keep it!" the Moon said, "I have more;
   Twelve new ones every year.
Ride in it with him every night, —
   The baby-brother dear!

"But tell him not to cry for me,
  Since I must walk my round
Through my great nursery of stars:
  So let his sleep be sound!

"And I will kiss him every night
  As I am passing by.
And you two, in your silver sledge,
  May chase me through the sky."

Girl-Peepsy rubbed her dazzled eyes;
  "I thank you, Lady Moon!
I think the baby's not awake,
  I have come back so soon."

She rubbed her eyes: the baby slept.—
  A strange thing does it seem
That Peepsy went and brought the moon?
  She did it in a dream.

IN THE TREE-TOP.

"ROCK-A-BY, baby, up in the tree-top!"
  Mother his blanket is spinning;
And a light little rustle that never will stop,
  Breezes and boughs are beginning.
Rock-a-by, baby, swinging so high!
        Rock-a-by!

"When the wind blows, then the cradle will rock."
 Hush! now it stirs in the bushes;
Now with a whisper, a flutter of talk,
 Baby and hammock it pushes.
Rock-a-by, baby! shut, pretty eye!
   Rock-a-by!

"Rock with the boughs, rock-a-by, baby, dear!"
 Leaf-tongues are singing and saying;
Mother she listens, and sister is near,
 Under the tree softly playing.
Rock-a-by, baby! mother's close by!
   Rock-a-by!

Weave him a beautiful dream, little breeze!
 Little leaves, nestle around him!
He will remember the song of the trees,
 When age with silver has crowned him.
Rock-a-by, baby! wake by and by!
   Rock-a-by!

BABY'S DAY.

OPEN your eyes, mamma;
Day soon will begin.
Open your eyes, mamma!
I want to look in.
Yesterday, dear mamma,
Out of your eyes
There peeped two little boys
Just of my size.

Are they in there now, mamma?
Whose can they be?
And do you love those boys
As you love me?

Don't feed me any longer, —
　Not another minute!
Does my mouth look pretty, think,
　With a great spoon in it?

If you people speak the
　　truth,
　I am sweet enough;
There's no need of chok-
　　ing me
　With your sugary stuff.

Mamma, where are you?
　You are the sweet!
Nicer than all
　They can give me to eat.
Here I am coming, —
　Toes, fingers, and feet!
Have you a kiss or two
　Growing for me?

Where do you hide them?
Please let me see!
Now I shall steal them, —
One, two, and three.

What is the next thing
 For baby to do?
Duckie, I think,
 I 'll go swimming with
  you.

Doggie, look sharp,
And if we get drowned,
Fish us both out,
You friendly old hound!

Dick, we 'll on our travels go,
I 've two feet, don't hold me so!
O, my shoes won't walk a bit!
Down upon the floor I 'll sit.
If you think I 've had a fall,
You 're mistaken, that is all!

But why will this old house shake,
Every single step I take?

Now get out my pony, Dick!
Whoa! gee up there! where's my stick?

Over the world and away
to the moon,
Clever old Dick, we must
get there soon,
Or the barley-candy will all
be sold,
And we can't buy a gingerbread horse for gold.

O, the sand blows in my eye,
Here is Noddy's Isle close by;

And, — don't tell me that
I fib! —
Dick, it looks just like my
crib.

Good night, pony! Trot away!
I 've done riding for to-day,
And I hear my mother sing,
Sweet, O, sweet as anything! —

My baby shall go
  To the Island of Sleep,
Where soft little dream-waves
  Around him will creep.
And when the moon rises,
  Away in her boat,
With the stars rowing races
  All night he shall float.
And when morning's red horses
  Spring out of the sea,
As swift as a sunbeam
  He 'll come back to me.

THE BABY'S THOUGHTS.

" I WONDER what the baby thinks.
    Just see how wide awake she lies,
And crows at me, and chirps, and winks,
    With laughing wonder in her eyes."

I'll answer for her, little girl. —
    "Whose can it be, that merry face,
With hair like sunbeams in a curl,
    That hangs around my nestling-place?

"At three months old I've much to learn,
    For everything looks strange to me.
But then I know enough to turn
    To all the brightest things I see.

"Red roses on the curtain grow,
　　Once, when 't was up, I saw a star.
I wonder, Brown Eyes, if you know
　　How many splendid things there are?

"Now don't you wish you were n't so tall?
　　Then you 'd live in a cradle, too,
And talk to shadows on the wall,
　　And think you heard them talk to you.

"But, then, I could n't spare you, dear;
　　For when I wake from pretty dreams,
And that great sun goes by, so near,
　　You seem like one of his soft beams.

"I guess that you, and mother too,
　　Are pieces broken from the sun.
No; she's the sun, a sunbeam you;
　　For when she goes, away you run.

THE BABY'S THOUGHTS.

"I lie here guessing every day
  What all the things around can be;
This four-walled world in which I stay
  Is full of wonders, dear, to me." —

There, little girl, your sunny face
  Will give the baby thoughts like these;
Then let no frown your brow disgrace,
  But be the loveliest thing she sees.

MOONSHINE.

LITTLE pet sat in the moonshine,
    A square of light on the floor,
Shaped by the open window;
    And its halo dim he wore.

It turned his hair to spun silver,
    His robe into folds of pearl;
Yet it was but a linen nightgown,
    A tangle of flaxen curl.

He was there at play, white nestling!
    A moment before he slept;
And he patted and kissed the moonbeams,
    And, cooing, across them crept.

MOONSHINE.

"Bring us the moonshine, baby!"
  Quick sprang the little feet;
Scooping it up by lapfuls,
  Hurried the fingers sweet,

To load us with unseen treasure.
  He saw it, bright and plain;
Never doubted the baby
  Ours was a real gain.

Firmly we also believed it;
  For, after he was asleep,
We had his moonlit picture
  Always our own to keep.

It has not grown old, or faded;
  It will not, it never can.
We shall have it still to look at
  When he is a bearded man.

If then he should win great riches,
  He cannot bestow a gift
So rare as the one he brought us
  Out of the moonbeams' drift.

May he never lose faith in moonshine, —
  The ore that glimmers and streams
From the mountain-clefts of beauty,
  In the far-off world of dreams!

Right royally may he scatter
  The wealth of unfathomed skies, —
The fine gold and sheeny silver
  From the mines of Paradise.

HAL'S BIRTHDAY.

FOUR years old when the blackberries come!
   After the roses have blossomed and gone,
And you only hear the wild-bee's hum
   In the bough that the robin sang upon.

Columbines will not nod from the rock,
   Nor blue-eyed violets hide in the grass,
Nor the wind with the sweet-breathed clover talk,
   When pussy and I down the meadow pass.

But she will run after me, all the same,
   With her spotted back and her frisky tail,
And will stop and look when I call her name,
   Or spring at my curls from the high fence-rail.

Cherries and strawberries, you may go;
  We shall not fret about you in the least,
Out where the plump, sweet blackberries grow, —
  Pussy and I, at my birthday feast.

If there's a grasshopper left in sight,
  Or a locust spinning his long, dry tune,
They are the guests that we will invite.
  To eat with us in the shade at noon.

Overhead will the sky be blue,
  And the grass we tread will be short and green,
And a late field-daisy — one or two —
  Will, may be, among the vines be seen.

And perhaps, perhaps I shall go to the wood.
   Where the pines bend down to the feathery ferns,
And the cardinal-flowers bloom as red as blood,
   And the moss to gold in the sunshine turns.

And there I shall gather my basket full
   Of fragrant clethra as white as snow,
And partridge-berries and club-moss pull,
   And play by the pond where the lilies grow.

Mother, and all of us, pussy, too,
   Will eat our supper under the trees,
Before it is time for the sunset dew;
   Then loiter homeward, slow as we please, —

Watching the squirrels peep from the wall,
   Mocking the whistle of scared chewink,
Hearing the cows for the milkers call; —
   Pleasant our walk will be, I think.

Months of summer will soon pass by;
    Time slips along, who is guessing how?
Fast and faster the merry days fly, —
    But don't you wish it was August now?

A HAREBELL.

MOTHER, if I were a flower
  Instead of a little child,
 I would choose my home by a waterfall,
  To laugh at its gambols wild, —
   To be sprinkled with spray and dew; —
   And I'd be a harebell blue.

Blue is the color of heaven,
 And blue is the color for me.
But in the rough earth my clinging roots
 Closely nestled should be;
  For the earth is friendly and true
  To the little harebell blue.

I could not look up to the sun
    As the bolder blossoms look;
But he would look up with a smile to me
    From his mirror in the brook,
        And his smile would thrill me through, —
        A trembling harebell blue.

The winds would not break my stem
    When they rushed in tempest by;
I would bend before them, for they come
    From the loving Hand on high,
        That never a harm can do
        To a slender harebell blue.

I would play with shadow and breeze;
    I would blossom from June till frost.
Dear mother, I know you would find me out,
    When my stream-side cliff you crossed,
        And I'd give myself to you, —
        Your own little harebell blue.

SIR ROBIN.

ROLLICKING Robin is here again.
What does he care for the April rain?
Care for it? Glad of it. Does n't he know
That the April rain carries off the snow,
And coaxes out leaves to shadow his nest,
And washes his pretty red Easter vest,
And makes the juice of the cherry sweet,
For his hungry little robins to eat?

"Ha! ha! ha!" hear the jolly bird laugh.
"That isn't the best of the story, by half!"

Gentleman Robin, he walks up and down,
Dressed in orange-tawny and black and brown.
Though his eye is so proud and his step so firm,
He can always stoop to pick up a worm.
With a twist of his head, and a strut and a hop,
To his Robin-wife, in the peach-tree top,
Chirping her heart out, he calls: "My dear,
You don't earn your living! Come here! Come here!
Ha! ha! ha! Life is lovely and sweet;
But what would it be if we'd nothing to eat?"

Robin, Sir Robin, gay, red-vested knight,
Now you have come to us, summer's in sight.
You never dream of the wonders you bring, —
Visions that follow the flash of your wing.
How all the beautiful By-and-by
Around you and after you seems to fly!

Sing on, or eat on, as pleases your mind!
Well have you earned every morsel you find.
"Aye! Ha! ha! ha!" whistles Robin. "My dear,
Let us all take our own choice of good cheer!"

GOWNS OF GOSSAMER.

THEY 're hastening up across the fields; I see them on their way!
They will not wait for cloudless skies, nor even a pleasant day;
For Mother Earth will weave and spread a carpet for their feet;
Already voices in the air announce their coming sweet.

One sturdy little violet peeped out alone, in March,
While cobwebs of the snow yet hung about the sky's gray arch;
But merry winds to sweep them down in earnest had begun:
The violet, though she shook with cold, stayed on to watch the fun.

And now the other violets are crowding up to see
What welcome in this blustering world may chance for
    them to be :
They lift themselves on slender stems in every shaded
    place, —
Heads over heads, all turned one way, wonder in every
    face.

There shiver, in rose-tinted white, the pale anemones ;
There pink, perfumed arbutus trails from underneath bare
    trees ;
Hepatica shows opal gleams beneath her silk-lined cloak,
Then slips it off, and hides amid the gnarled roots of
    the oak.

They like the clear, cool weather well, when they are
    fairly out,
And they are happy as the flowers of sunnier climes, no
    doubt.

When little star-shaped innocence makes every field snow-white
With her four-cornered neckerchiefs, there is no lovelier sight.

And when the wild geranium comes, in gauzy purple sheen,
Forerunner of the woodland rose, June's darling, Summer's queen,
With small herb-robert like a page close following her feet,
Jack-in-the-pulpit will stand up in his green-curtained seat:

Marsh-marigold and adder's-tongue will wade the brook across,
Where cornel-flowers are grouped, in crowds, on strips of turf and moss;
And wood-stars white, from lucent green will glimmer and unfold,
And scarlet columbines will lift their trumpets, mouthed with gold.

Then will the birds sing anthems; for the earth and sky
 and air
Will seem a great cathedral, filled with beings dear and
 fair;
And long processions, from the time that bluebird-notes
 begin
Till gentians fade, through forest-aisles will still move
 out and in.

Unnumbered multitudes of flowers it were in vain to
 name,
Along the roads and in the woods will old acquaintance
 claim;
And scarcely shall we know which one for beauty we
 prefer
Of all the wayside fairies clad in gowns of gossamer.

CALLING THE VIOLET.

DEAR little Violet,
 Don't be afraid!
Lift your blue eyes
 From the rock's mossy shade!

CALLING THE VIOLET.

All the birds call for you
   Out of the sky :
May is here, waiting,
   And here, too, am I.

Why do you shiver so,
   Violet sweet?
Soft is the meadow-grass
   Under my feet.
Wrapped in your hood of green,
   Violet, why
Peep from your earth-door
   So silent and shy?

Trickle the little brooks
   Close to your bed;
Softest of fleecy clouds
   Float overhead;
"Ready and waiting!"
   The slender reeds sigh:

"Ready and waiting!"
   We sing — May and I.

Come, pretty Violet,
   Winter's away:
Come, for without you
   May is n't May.
Down through the sunshine
   Wings flutter and fly; —
Quick, little Violet,
   Open your eye!

Hear the rain whisper,
   "Dear Violet, come!"
How can you stay
   In your underground home?
Up in the pine-boughs
   For you the winds sigh.
Homesick to see you,
   Are we — May and I.

Ha! though you care not
  For call or for shout,
Yon troop of sunbeams
  Are winning you out.
Now all is beautiful
  Under the sky:
May's here, — and violets!
  Winter, good by!

THE RIVULET.

RUN, little rivulet, run!
　　Summer is fairly begun.
Bear to the meadow the hymn of the pines,
And the echo that rings where the water-
　　　　fall shines;
　　Run, little rivulet, run!

　　Run, little rivulet, run!
　　Sing to the fields of the sun

That wavers in emerald, shimmers in gold,
Where you glide from your rocky ravine, crystal-cold;
    Run, little rivulet, run!

    Run, little rivulet, run!
    Sing of the flowers, every one, —
Of the delicate harebell and violet blue;
Of the red mountain rose-bud, all dripping with dew;
    Run, little rivulet, run!

    Run, little rivulet, run!
    Carry the perfume you won
From the lily, that woke when the morning was gray,
To the white waiting moonbeam adrift on the bay;
    Run, little rivulet, run!

    Run, little rivulet, run!
    Stay not till summer is done!
Carry the city the mountain-birds' glee;
Carry the joy of the hills to the sea;
    Run, little rivulet, run!

THE BROWN THRUSH.

THERE's a merry brown thrush sitting up in the tree.
"He's singing to me! He's singing to me!"
And what does he say, little girl, little boy?
"O, the world's running over with joy!
Don't you hear? Don't you see?
Hush! Look! In my tree
I'm as happy as happy can be!"

THE BROWN THRUSH.

And the brown thrush keeps singing, " A nest do you see,
    And five eggs, hid by me in the juniper-tree?
Don't meddle! don't touch! little girl, little boy,
    Or the world will lose some of its joy!
        Now I'm glad! now I'm free!
            And I always shall be,
If you never bring sorrow to me."

So the merry brown thrush sings away in the tree,
    To you and to me, to you and to me;
And he sings all the day, little girl, little boy,
    " O, the world's running over with joy!
        But long it won't be,
            Don't you know? don't you see?
Unless we are as good as can be?"

SPRING WHISTLES.

DOWN by the gate of the orchard
    This Saturday afternoon,
Harry and Arthur and Willie
    Are getting their whistles in tune.
Different notes they are playing;
    Different echoes they hear:
Always the best of the music
    Is in the musician's ear.

Harry says, "Hark! when I whistle,
    March winds are wild on the hills;
Waterfalls break from the snow-drifts;
    Their thunder the forest fills.
Thousands of bluebirds and sparrows
    Sing on the branches bare;

SPRING WHISTLES.

Oceans of musical murmurs
  Ripple and stir in the air."

Arthur is whispering, " Listen !
  Dropping of April showers, —
Dripping of rainy rosebuds, —
  Flight of the rustling hours ; —
And a speckled lark in the meadow,
  That utters one long sad note,
As if all the sorrow of gladness
  Were hid in his little throat."

" Whistle, O whistle ! " cries Willie.
  " Never such echoes could be
Coaxed from a twig of the willow
  As wait in my whistle for me.
When I shape at last the mouth-piece
  And let the rich music out,
You will think that Pan or Apollo
  Is wandering hereabout:

"You will dream of orchards in blossom,
    Of lambs in the grass at play;
And of birds that warble all summer
    The wonderful songs of May."
No doubt of it, Will! in the whistle
    That nobody yet has played,
Is sleeping a melody sweeter
    Than ever on earth was made.

PLAYTHINGS.

NOT much to make us happy
　　Do any of us need;
But just the right thing give us,
　　And we are rich indeed.

Even as with men and women
　　It is with girls and boys.
Why should you shower on Jeanie
　　So many dear-bought toys?

Some bits of broken china,
　　A handful of corn-floss,
A shred or two of ribbon,
　　A strip of velvet moss;

With her family of rag-children,
    And the wide clean earth around, —
No happier little housewife
    Can anywhere be found.

But Nannie dear would rather
    Leave Jeanie to her play,
And wander by the streamlet,
    Or on the hill-top stray.

For a little white cloud passing,
    A ripple on the brook,
Much more her heart enriches
    Than play-house, doll, or book.

Half Nannie's wealth lies hidden
    Under the rock's green shelf:
You cannot find it for her;
    She keeps the key herself.

Wild John likes forest-freedom,
   And room for boundless noise,
Better than spending-money
   Or a city-full of toys.

And small Ned with a shingle
   Digs in his heap of sand;
Never swayed Inca sceptre
   Upon a throne so grand.

With large and little children
   The trouble is the same:
What pleases us, to others
   Is wearisome and tame.

Good friends, your entertainment
   A well-meant plan may be;
But he's our benefactor
   Who simply leaves us free.

Gipsy Children's Song

WHITE little housed-up things,
Why don't you run
Out in the sun?
Beauty that blossoms and sings
Never was made
Strong in the shade.

GIPSY CHILDREN'S SONG.

Why do you shadow the face
    Pale as a doll's,
    Now the wind calls,
"Hurry, and give us a chase"?
    Where the winds blow
    Roses will grow.

Here we swing high on the bough!
    Down comes the rain,
    Blackberry stain
Washing from bare cheek and brow,
    Fresh as a flower
    After the shower.

We and the pine-trees are glad
    When the winds talk
    Through a split rock
Till they go merrily mad,
    Making us shake, —
    Laugh till we ache.

Then in the warm lull of noon
    Sleepy we slide
    Down the rill-side,
Dropping away to its tune
    Into a dream
    Bright as the stream.

Always at home with you, Sun! —
    Mother, so high
    Up in the sky,
Smiling out full on our fun, —
    Paint us with tan
    Brown as you can!

O little housed-up things!
    Blue is the air,
    Breezy and fair;
Borrow a bird's idle wings;
    Then you may be
    Merry as we!

MANITOU'S GARDEN.

"COME, play in my garden!"
    Called flaxen-haired Fred,
Peeping out from the edge
    Of a hyacinth-bed,
Through the stout oaken rails
    At a Chippewa boy
Who ran along, dragging
    A snake, for a toy.

"I'll give you some flowers
    To twist in your hair."
"The son of a sachem
    No blossoms will wear
That the white man has planted;
    Nor yet will he go

Where roses and lilies
   Like pale captives grow.

"In Manitou's garden
   Are gay flowers to see:
Come out, little pale-face,
   And play here with me!
The fawn will play with us, —
   The squirrel and hare;
No fences to stop us, —
   We 're free as the air.

"In Manitou's garden
   How bright is the dawn!
We know where his trail
   Through the deer-path has gone.
The moccasin-flower
   Springs up where he stopped;
And the dewdrops are beads,
   From his blanket's edge dropped."

"I 'm afraid, little Indian,
　　To come out to you.
I 'm afraid of the snakes,
　　And the barking wolves, too."
"Ugh! white-hearted pale-face,
　　They 're Manitou's snakes;
And the wolves are the hounds
　　That a-hunting he takes.

"We, too, on wild mustangs
　　Chase bisons and deer.
We are Manitou's hunters,
　　A race without fear.
Our arrow's flight leaves
　　The swift eagle behind.
Whoop! after them, quick
　　As the rushing north-wind!"

But the son of the Chippewa
　　Stands there alone,

At his whoop timid Fred
To his mother has flown.
Off the red boy runs, shouting,
"Whoop! whoop! let him be!
In Manitou's garden
Are playmates for me!"

DUMPY DUCKY.

QUACK, quack, quack!
Three white and four black.
Your coat, you saucy fellow,
Shades off to green and yellow:
    Do you think I like you best
    Because you are prettiest?

Quack, quack, quack!
White spots on his back,
Chasing his long-necked brothers,
I see him, old duck-mothers;—
    You need not quack so loud,
    Nor look so stiff and proud.

Quack, quack, quack!
Ducks, you have a knack
Of talking and saying nothing,
And showing off fine clothing
Like many folks I see
Who wiser ought to be.

Quack, quack, quack!
Please to stop your clack!
They call me Dumpy Ducky;
Do you not think you are lucky,
You ducklings all, to be
Named for a girl like me?

Quack, quack, quack!
What is there that we lack, —
You with a pond for swimming,
I with my bucket brimming, —
You with your web-toes neat,
I with my stout bare feet?

DUMPY DUCKY.

Quack, quack, quack!
You make a funny track
When you waddle through the garden.
And, ducks, I beg your pardon,
    But I do not choose to try
    A swim in your pond; not I!

Quack, quack, quack!
Now you may all turn back,
Your home is in the water;
I am the Dutchman's daughter,
    And my plump little sisters cry,
    "We want a drink!" Good b'ye!

PUSSY-CLOVER.

PUSSY-CLOVER 's running wild,
　　Here and there and anywhere,
Like a little vagrant child
　　Free of everybody's care.

All unshaded roadsides know
　　Pussy-Clover's sunburnt head,
That by cabin door-steps low
　　Lifts itself in tawny red.

Lady-Rose is shy and proud;
　　Maiden-Lily bashful-sweet:
Pussy-Clover loves a crowd, —
　　Seeks the paths of hurrying feet.

When tow-headed children run
   Jostling to the railway track,
Pussy-Clover 's in the fun,
   Nodding forward, nodding back.

Matters little who sits there,
   In the thundering car swept by;
Blossoms bow, and children stare,
   Neither offering reason why.

Downy heads to hoary turn;
   Scarcely noted is the change:
But the fair world's face grows stern, —
   Wayside blossoms wan and strange.

Like all faithful, homely things,
   Pussy-clover lingers on
Till the bird no longer sings,
   And the butterfly is gone.

When the latest asters go,
    When the golden-rod drops dead,
Then, at last, in heaps of snow
    Pussy-Clover hides her head.

BERRYING SONG.

HO! for the hills in summer!
  Ho! for the rocky shade,
Where the groundpine trails under the fern-leaves,
  Deep in the mossy glade.
Up in the dewy sunrise,
  Waked by the robin's trill;
Up and away, a-berrying,
  To the pastures on the hill!

Red lilies blaze out of the thicket;
   Wild roses blush here and there:
There's sweetness in all the breezes,
   There's health in each breath of air.
Hark to the wind in the pine-trees!
   Hark to the tinkling rill!
O, pleasant it is a-berrying
   In the pastures on the hill!

We'll garland our baskets with blossoms,
   And sit on the rocks and sing,
And tell one another old stories,
   Till the trees long shadows fling.
Then homeward with laughter and carol,
   Mocking the echoes shrill.
O, merry it is a-berrying
   In the pastures on the hill!

SWINGING ON A BIRCH-TREE.

SWINGING on a birch-tree
   To a sleepy tune,
Hummed by all the breezes
   In the month of June!
Little leaves a-flutter
   Sound like dancing drops
Of a brook on pebbles, —
   Song that never stops.

Up and down we seesaw:
   Up into the sky;
How it opens on us,
   Like a wide blue eye!
You and I are sailors
   Rocking on a mast;

And the world's our vessel:
　Ho! she sails so fast!

Blue, blue sea around us;
　Not a ship in sight;
They will hang out lanterns
　When they pass, to-night.
We with ours will follow
　Through the midnight deep;
Not a thought of danger,
　Though the crew's asleep.

O, how still the air is!
　There an oriole flew;
What a jolly whistle!
　He's a sailor, too.
Yonder is his hammock
　In the elm-top high:
One more ballad, messmate!
　Sing it as you fly!

Up and down we seesaw;
  Down into the grass,
Scented fern, and rosebuds,
  All a woven mass.
That's the sort of carpet
  Fitted for our feet;
Tapestry nor velvet
  Is so rich and neat.

Swinging on a birch-tree!
  This is summer joy,
Fun for all vacation, —
  Don't you think so, boy?
Up and down to seesaw,
  Merry and at ease,
Careless as a brook is,
  Idle as the breeze.

LITTLE NANNIE.

FAWN-FOOTED Nannie,
    Where have you been?
"Chasing the sunbeams
    Into the glen;
Plunging through silver lakes
    After the moon;
Tracking o'er meadows
    The footsteps of June."

Sunny-eyed Nannie,
    What did you see?
"Saw the fays sewing
    Green leaves on a tree;
Saw the waves counting
    The eyes of the stars;

Saw cloud-lambs sleeping
    By sunset's red bars."

Listening Nannie,
    What did you hear?
" Heard the rain asking
    A rose to appear;
Heard the woods tell
    When the wind whistled wrong;
Heard the stream flow
    Where the bird drinks his song."

Nannie, dear Nannie,
    O, take me with you,
To run and to listen,
    And see as you do!
" Nay, nay! you must borrow
    My ear and my eye,
Or the beauty will vanish,
    The music will die."

A LILY'S WORD.

MY delicate lily, —
Blossom of fragrant snow,
Breathing on me from the garden,
How does your beauty grow?
Tell me what blessing the kind heavens give!
How do you find it so sweet to live?

"One loving smile of the sun
Charms me out of the mould:
One tender tear of the rain
Makes my full heart unfold,—
Welcome whatever the kind heavens give,
And you shall find it as sweet to live."

RED SANDWORT.

IT IS a little roadside flower,
Glad of leave to live an hour,
Just to wonder and to doubt
What the world can be about.

Tiniest rosy-purple stars
Strewn beneath the pasture-bars,
Or along the path, so small,
Few perceive a flower at all.

Burning sand and burning sun
This small blossom loves as one;
Well content in drawing thence
One short hour of light intense.

Opal rays it gathers up
In its tinted baby-cup,
Drinks and gives its draught of sun,
Then its pleasant life is done.

Opals are but sand refined;
These are gems, — a simpler kind;
All the light around they fling,
That can fill so small a thing.

Pretty sand-stars! ye have wrought
Round our feet a mesh of thought, —
Clinging to the wagon's track, —
Finding there nor loss nor lack, —

Happy in your patch of sand
As the rose in gardens grand; —
Happier, since a spot so bare
Feels your life, your tints can wear.

Just to live is joy enough,
Though where roads are dull and rough.
Fill your cup and share it! can
More be done by flower or man?

GRACE'S FRIENDS

"YOUR walk is lonely, blue-eyed Grace,
Down the long forest-road to school,

Where shadows troop, at dismal pace,
  From sullen chasm to sunless pool.
Are you not often, little maid,
Beneath the sighing trees afraid?"

"Afraid, — beneath the tall, strong trees,
  That bend their arms to shelter me,
And whisper down, with dew and breeze,
  Sweet sounds that float on lovingly,
Till every gorge and cavern seems
Thrilled through and through with fairy dreams?

"Afraid, — beside the water dim
  That holds the baby-lilies white
Upon its bosom, where a hymn
  Ripples forth softly to the light
That now and then comes gliding in,
A lily's budding smile to win?

"Fast to the slippery precipice
  I see the nodding harebell cling;

In that blue eye no fear there is ;
  Its hold is firm, — the frail, free thing !
The harebell's Guardian cares for me :
So I am in safe company.

" The woodbine clambers up the cliff
  And seems to murmur, ' Little Grace,
The sunshine were less welcome, if
  It brought not every day your face.'
Red leaves slip down from maples high,
And touch my cheek as they flit by.

" I feel at home with everything
  That has its dwelling in the wood ;
With flowers that laugh, and birds that sing, —
  Companions beautiful and good,
Brothers and sisters everywhere ;
And over all, our Father's care.

" In rose-time or in berry-time, —
  When ripe seeds fall, or buds peep out, —

While green the turf, or white the rime,
   There 's something to be glad about.
It makes my heart bound, just to pass
The sunbeams dancing on the grass.

"And when the bare rocks shut me in
   Where not a blade of grass will grow,
My happy fancies soon begin
   To warble music, rich and low,
And paint what eyes could never see:
My thoughts are company for me.

"What does it mean to be alone?
   And how is any one afraid,
Who feels the dear God on his throne
   Sending his sunshine through the shade,
Warming the damp sod into bloom
And smiling off the thicket's gloom?

"At morning, down the wood-path cool
   The fluttering leaves make cheerful talk;

After the stifled day at school,
  I hear, along my homeward walk,
The airy wisdom of the wood, —
Far easiest to be understood.

" I whisper to the winds ; I kiss
  The rough old oak and clasp his bark ;
No farewell of the thrush I miss ;
  I lift the soft veil of the dark,
And say to bird and breeze and tree,
' Good night ! Good friends you are to me ! ' "

THE BROOK THAT RAN INTO THE SEA.

"LITTLE brook," the children said,
  "The sea has waves enough;
Why hurry down your mossy bed
  To meet his welcome rough?

"The Hudson or the Oregon
  May help his tides to swell:
But when your few bright drops are gone,
  What has he gained, pray tell?"

"I run for pleasure," said the brook,
  Still running, running fast;

"I love to see you bend and look,
  As I go bubbling past.

"I love to feel the wild weeds dip;
  I love your fingers light,
That dimpling from my eddies drip,
  Filled with my pebbles bright.

"My own mysterious life I love,
  Its shadow and its shine;
And all sweet voices that above
  Make melody with mine.

"But most I love the mighty voice
  Which calls me, draws me so,
That every ripple lisps, 'Rejoice!'
  As with a laugh I go.

"My drop of freshness to the Sea
  In music trickles on;

Nor grander could my welcome be
　　Were I an Amazon.

"And if his moaning waves can feel
　　My sweetness near the shore,
Even to his heart the thrill may steal : —
　　What could I wish for more?

"The largest soul to take love in
　　Knows how to give love best;
So peacefully my tinkling din
　　Dies on the great Sea's breast.

"One heart encircles all that live,
　　And blesses great and small;
And meet it is that each should give
　　His little to the All."

THE LAST FLOWER OF THE YEAR.

THE gentian was the year's last child,
    Born when the winds were hoarse and wild
With wailing over buried flowers,
The playmates of their sunnier hours.

The gentian hid a thoughtful eye
Beneath dark fringes, blue and shy,
Only by warmest noon-beams won,
To meet the welcome of the sun.

The gentian, her long lashes through,
Looked up into the sky so blue,
And felt at home, — the color there
The good God gave herself to wear.

The gentian searched the fields around;
No flower-companion there she found.
Upward, from all the woodland ways
Floated the aster's silvery rays.

The gentian shut her eyelids tight
On falling leaf and frosty night;
And close her azure mantle drew,
While dreary winds around her blew.

The gentian said, "The world is cold;
Yet one clear glimpse of heaven I hold.
The sun's last thought is mine to keep;
Enough — now let me go to sleep."

JESSIE'S BOOK.

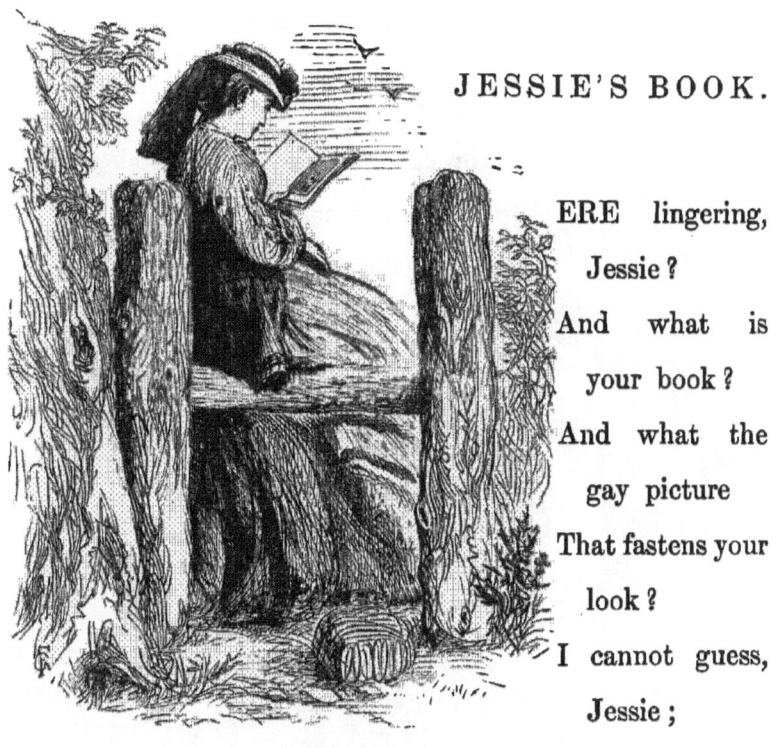

ERE lingering,
Jessie?
And what is
your book?
And what the
gay picture
That fastens your
look?
I cannot guess,
Jessie;
Still seems it to me
A lovelier picture
Your raised eyes would see.

The late birds are flying
   Through sunshine's soft floods;
Cool shadows are lying
   Beside the warm woods;
There are gentians and frost-flowers
   In dim dingles hid;
Sleeps beauty the bowers
   Of autumn amid.

To sit here and read
   On the pleasant old stile
Is a fine thing indeed;
   Yet those pages may wile
Your thoughts from a story
   More wonderful still,
That hangs a wild glory
   Round meadow and hill.

For Nature, dear Jessie,
   Has something to say

She will not say over
   Again, any day.
And if I were Jessie
   My book I would close,
And read the fresh marvels
   Her latest page shows.

When angry November
   Has torn the bright leaves,
You will not remember
   What tints Autumn weaves.
Go, con the blue river,
   The torrent, the brook,
Ere winter forever
   Seal up this year's book!

RED-TOP AND TIMOTHY.

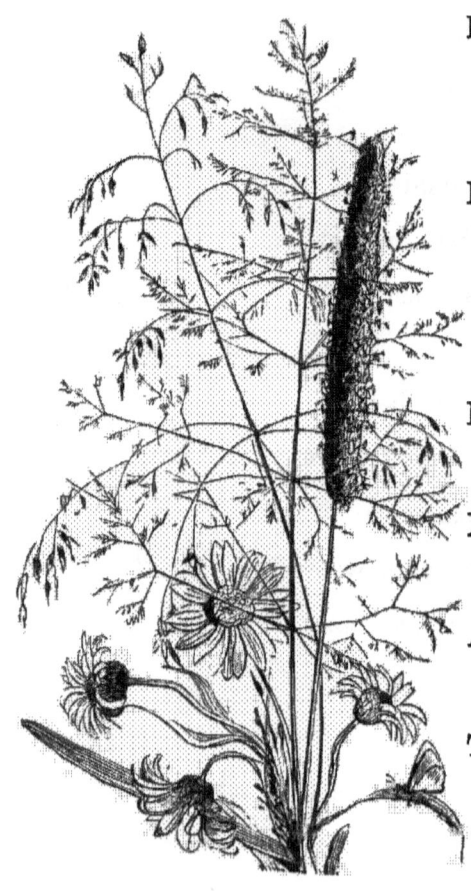

RED-TOP and Timothy
  Come here in the
    spring;
Light spears out of em-
    erald sheaths
  Everywhere they
    swing.
Harmless little soldiers,
  On the field they play,
Nodding plumes and
    crossing blades
All the livelong day.

Timothy and Red-Top
  Bring their music-
    band;

Some with scarlet epaulettes
  Strutting stiff and grand ;
Some in sky-blue jackets ;
  Some in vests of pink :
Black and white their leader's coat,
  Restless Bob-o'-link !

Red-Top's airy feathers
  Tremble to his notes,
In themselves an orchestra ;
  Then a thousand throats
Set the winds a-laughing,
  While the saucy thing
Anywhere, on spike or spear,
  Sways himself to sing.

Red-Top and Timothy
  Have a mortal foe ;
There's a giant with a scythe
  Comes and lays them low ;

Shuts them in barn-prisons;
  Spares not even Sweet Clover:
Bob-o'-link leads off his band,
  Now the campaign's over.

Timothy and Red-Top
  Will return again,
With familiar songs and flowers,
  Through the April rain.
Though their giant foeman
  Will not let them be,
One who swings a keener scythe
  Cuts down such as he.

FLOWER-GIRLS.

MY little seaside girl,
  What is in your garden growing?
"Rock-weeds and tangle-grass,
  With the slow tide coming, going;
Samphire and marsh-rosemary
  All along the wet shore creeping;
Sandwort, beach-peas, pimpernel,
  Out of nooks and corners peeping."

O my little prairie girl,
  What's in bloom among your grasses?

"Spring-beauties, painted cups,
  Flushing when the south-wind passes:
Beds of rose-pink centaury;

  Compass-flowers, to northward turning:
Larkspur, orange-gold puccoon;
  Leagues of lilies flame-red burning."

O my little mountain girl,
  Have you anything to gather?
"White-everlasting bloom,
  Not afraid of wind or weather;
Sweet-brier, leaning on the crag
  That the lady-fern hides under;
Harebells, violets white and blue:
  Who has sweeter flowers, I wonder?"

O my little maidens three,
  I will lay your pretty posies,
Sea-scented, cloud-bedewed,
  Prairie-grasses, mountain roses,
On a bed of shells and moss.
  Come and bend your bright heads nearer!
Though your blossoms are so fair,
  You three human flowers are dearer!

THE CLOCK-TINKER.

TINKER, may I learn the trick, —
　　How you cure a clock that's sick,
Peeping in her face behind,
(Are those wheels her brains?) to find
Why her pulses do not go
Regular and sure and slow?

Tinker, have you learned Time's trick, —
How it is he makes clocks tick?
Is there such a thing as knowing
What it was first set them going?
Do you, sir, suppose they had 'em
In their garden, Eve and Adam?

Is there, up among the suns, —
Father of these other ones, —
Some great timepiece that can show
All the small clocks how to go?
Are the stars set right by some
Mighty swinging pendulum?

Tinker, where's the loosened screw
That the juggler Time creeps through
When he slips into his place,
Up behind the old clock's face?
Have you ever seen that feat?
Or does Time even graybeards cheat?

"Boy, I've tried through Time to see,
But he played strange tricks with me.
While I gave the wizard chase,
He was dancing on my face.
Look you! like a crow he flies;
Here's his track around my eyes."

CAT-QUESTIONS.

DOZING, and dozing, and dozing!
    Pleasant enough,
Dreaming of sweet cream and mouse-meat, —
    Delicate stuff!

Of raids on the pantry and hen-coop,—
    Or light, stealthy tread
Of cat-gossips, meeting by moonlight
    On ridge-pole or shed. —

Waked by a somerset, whirling
    From cushion to floor;
Waked to a wild rush for safety
    From window to door.

Waking to hands that first smooth us,
    And then pull our tails;
Punished with slaps when we show them
    The length of our nails!

These big mortal tyrants even grudge us
    A place on the mat.

Do they think we enjoy for our music
    Staccatoes of " scat " ?

What in the world were we made for?
    Man, do you know?
By you to be petted, tormented? —
    Are *you* friend or foe?

To be treated, now, just as you treat us, —
    The question is pat, —
To take just our chances in living,
    Would *you* be a cat?

A FACE IN THE TONGS.

A CHILD'S round face in the tongs;
    She is rubbing the brasses bright,
While merry old-fashioned nursery-songs
    She croons with a child's delight.

She sees in the glittering sphere
    Her broadened baby-face
Smiling back on itself with a wordless cheer,
    And filling the globe-like space.

Little friend, by my name once known,
    I am rubbing the tongs to-day;
But the face that I gaze on you would not own,
    It has lost your child-look gay

O, your world was golden and glad:
   Your happy heart was enough,
Though that and the sunshine were all you had,
   And earth underfoot was rough.

But one thing I learned from you
   I have not forgotten, quite;
No pleasanter work can a mortal do
   Than to keep one small world bright.

And, thinking about you, dear,
   The face in the tongs has smiled.
In a dream I went back to your shining sphere,
   And played with myself, a child.

THE BARN WINDOW.

THE old barn window, John, —
  Do you remember it, —
How just above it, on the beam,
  The tame doves used to sit,
And how we watched the sunshine stream
  Through motes and gossamer,
When down they fluttered, John,
  With such a breezy whirr?

I think the sunsets, John,
  Are seldom now as red;

They used to linger like a crown
    Upon your auburn head.
From the high hayloft looking down
    To tell me of the nest
The white hen hid there, John, —
    The whole brood's handsomest!

Those times were pleasant, John,
    When we were boy and girl,
Though modern young folk style them "slow";
    Alack! a giddy whirl
The poor old world is spinning now,
    To stop, who guesses when?
Be thankful with me, John,
    That we were children then!

Have you forgotten, John,
    That Wednesday afternoon
When the great doors were opened wide,
    And all the scents of June

Came in to greet us, side by side,
    In the high-seated swing,
Where flocks of swallows, John,
    Fanned us with startled wing?

Up to the barn eaves, John,
    We swung, two happy things,
At home and careless in the air
    As if we both had wings.
The mountain-side lay far and fair,
    Beyond the blue stream's shore;
I cried, "Swing higher, John!"
    And fell upon the floor.

Next time I saw you, John,
    You stood beside my bed;
Tears trembled in your clear boy-glance, —
    I thought that I was dead,
But felt my childish pulses dance
    To be beside you still:

I lived to love you, John,
    As to the end I will.

We swing no longer, John;
    We sit at our own door,
And watch the shadows on the hill,
    The sunshine on the shore.
But the window in the barn is still
    A magic-glass to me;
For through its cobwebs, John,
    Our childhood's days I see.

A LITTLE CAVALIER.

WHEN I was very young, indeed,
  Ages ago, my dear,
I had to stand by me at need
  A little cavalier;
The prettiest lad I ever met,
  Black-eyed, red-cheeked, and fat.
His face I never can forget.
  His name? Well — it was Nat.

I saw him first one pleasant day,
  Beside his mother's door.
His third year had not slipped away,
  And I was scarcely four.
Upon his arm a wooden gun
  He bore right soldierly;
I know not which it was first won
  My heart, that gun or he.

There never was a clumsier trap
  By child of mortal seen.
A button at its side went — snap!
  The gun was painted green.
But, shouldering it with martial tread,
  Proudest of girls was I;
While like a flag above his head
  Would my pink bonnet fly.

For Nat I gathered currants fine,
  And flowers that bloomed around;

Though only yellow celandine
   And blue gill-over-the-ground
Grew underneath the gray stone-wall;
   Still they retain their charm, —
Those homely blossoms which recall
   That early sunshine warm.

I never tasted gingerbread,
   Or doughnuts crisp and new,
But in my mother's ear I said:
   "For little Nat some, too."
The days were dull and dark when him
   To school I could not lead.
That love like ours at last grew dim
   A pity seems, indeed.

To me he brought no cake or toy;
   But then you know, my dear,
That he was nothing but a boy,
   And boys have ways so queer!

They do not stop to think of things
    That give us girls delight;
But take the best that fortune brings
    As if it were their right.

'T was no such trifle made us part.
    He loved my gifts to take,
And it was comfort to my heart
    To see him eat my cake.
It happened thus: One afternoon,
    As from the school we came, —
The day was sultry, late in June,
    Our faces both aflame, —

Beneath the blooming locust-trees
    We loitered, I and Nat;
His hair was lifted by the breeze,
    I firmly held his hat
By its long bridle-string of green,
    And lightly held his hand:

A LITTLE CAVALIER.

No happier tiny twain were seen
    Than we, in all the land.

A freckled girl was passing by,
    And down she gazed at me,
As if we children, Nat and I,
    Were something strange to see.
I looked at him and looked at her;
    Why did she scan us so?
The cruel words she uttered were:
    "I guess you've got a beau!"

"A beau! What! he?" At once I dropped
    The little hand and hat,
And home I ran, and never stopped
    Till I lost sight of Nat.
A beau! Some monstrous thing, no doubt,
    All tusks and fangs and claws;
The one they read to me about
    A *boa-constrictor* was.

None did I with my grief annoy;
   None should my terror know;
But, O, I wondered if a boy,
   Must always be a beau!
And so my happy days were done.
   That innocent-looking Nat,
The owner of that darling gun,
   How came *he* to be *that?*

Nat's doorstep nevermore I sought.
   No sign of woe gave he;
Much more of him I doubtless thought
   Than ever he of me.
Forgetting is not hard, for men
   As young as he, my dear,
And so I lost him there and then, —
   My little cavalier.

IN FAIRY-LAND.

 LITTLE knight and little maid
    Met on the rim of Fairy-Land.
A rippling stream betwixt them played.
    The little knight reached out his hand,

And said, "Now may I cross to you,
    Or will you come across to me?"
Out spoke the little maiden true:
    "Sir Knight, nor this nor that can be:

"For I am here white flowers to sow,
    That little maidens far behind,
Or wandering on the plains below,
    Their pathway up the hill may find:

"And you are there good work to do, —
  To clear the brambles from the way,
That little knights who follow you
  May not upon the mountains stray.

"But see! the stream, as up we climb,
  Is narrowing to a rivulet.
Hark! airy bells above us chime,
  And nearer every hour we get.

"Up where the fountain falls in gold
  It lies, — the cool, sweet Fairy-Land,
Where child-hearts never can grow old;
  And we will walk there, hand in hand.

"And in that country strange and blest,
  We'll find some lovely work to do
For many an earth-bewildered guest, —
  For wearier folk than I or you.

IN FAIRY-LAND.

"And upward, upward as we go,
  The fairy-secret we shall guess, —
The secret that we almost know, —
  Of living other hearts to bless.

"Sweet voices call us through the air;
  New languages we understand.
Is this our own world, grown so fair?
  Sir Knight, we are in Fairy-Land!"

SISTER AND BLUEBIRDS.

THE bluebirds, the bluebirds,
   Are out there in the snow;
The meaning of their music
   No heedless ear may know.
The violet's forerunner
   Is that faint bud of song,
And after it the harebells
   Will troop, a blue-eyed throng.

They drift their fluttering azure
   Across the snow-sheets white;
And underneath, the daisies
   Are stirring toward the light.

And soon the purple crane-bill
   And golden buttercup
For overbrimming sunshine
   Will hold their goblets up.

The bluebirds, the bluebirds!
   'T is but the fifth of March,
Yet, though there hangs no tassel
   On alder, birch, or larch,
They never have deceived us:
   If summer always came
Too slowly for our wishes,
   Their song was not to blame.

This earliest May-day herald,
   This prophet of the spring
Has brought celestial color
   Upon his breezy wing.
Heaven loves to scatter earthward
   Flakes of its own soft hue;

The first bird, the last blossom,
    Wear the same shade of blue.

The bluebirds, the bluebirds!
    We heard them through the snow,
When we were baby playmates,
    A long, long time ago.
Our birthday slid in music
    Down the sky's reddening arch;
We came here with the bluebirds,
    'Mid snow and song, in March.

The world slips through its changes,
    And we change year by year;
But childhood lives within us
    Forever fresh and dear.
All miracles and visions
    That used the earth to fill,
When life was one great sunrise,
    Are in the bluebird's trill.

FARTHER ON.

WE two went Maying up the hill,—
  Our little Hal and I,—
Led onward by a linnet's trill;
The wind was soft, the sea was still,
  And violet-blue the sky.

And blue as glimpses of the sea
  Shone level violet-beds,
Far down below bare crag and tree;

And, sweetly shy as flowers can be,
    White wind-flowers hung their heads.

Great crowds of scarlet columbines
    Made sunrise in the wood,
Against the darkness of the pines;
In lilac gauze amid green vines
    The wild geraniums stood.

There are no hillsides pleasanter
    Than ours, far on in May;
Light sea-winds leaf and blossom stir,
Never grew wood-flowers lovelier,
    And yet I could not stay.

Some strange bewildering of the hour
    My restless footsteps won;
Some whisper from a pine-tree bower,
Some fragrance of an unseen flower
    A little farther on.

Till, on a summit gray with moss
    I found myself alone;
And saw, the billowy woods across,
The ocean-billows foam and toss,
    And heard from both one moan.

What had I gained by climbing there?
    The flowers were pale and thin
Around my feet; but all the air
Held hints of unknown sweetness rare,
    Hid sky and wave within.

My boy-mate bounded up the steep,
    His lithe arms heaped with bloom, —
A treasure for a day to keep.
Saw he that grand horizon sweep,
    That glory of vast room?

I know not; but his flowers were bright,
    And full of perfume, too,

And he had felt a keen delight
In every sound and smell and sight;
　The cheerful woodland through.

Yet hope I that he may not rest
　In earthly sweetness won;
Since we in seeking are most blest,
And life hides evermore its best
　A little farther on.

SWING AWAY.

WING away,
    From the great cross-beam,
Hid in heaps of clover-hay,
    Scented like a dream.

    Higher yet!
Up, between the eaves,
Where the gray doves cooing flit
    Through the sun-gilt leaves.

Here we go!
Whistle, merry wind!
'T is a long day you must blow,
Lighter hearts to find.

Swing away!
Sweep the rough barn floor;
Looking through on Arcady
Framed in by the door!

One, two, three!
Quick! the round red sun,
Hid behind yon twisted tree,
Means to end the fun.

Swing away,
Over husks and grain!
Shall we ever be as gay,
If we swing again?

THE ROADSIDE PREACHER.

A MEMORY.

DEAD, is he — in a pauper's bed,
    The good old Larkin Moore?
Was there no place for that white head,
    None but the workhouse floor?
O, bear him out with reverent tread,
    Under blue heaven once more!

He came and went across our youth
    Like some arisen saint.
He flung his random dart of truth
    In fashion wild and quaint:
His figure and his garb, in sooth,
    Were something strange to paint.

His tunic fluttered in the wind;
    Each thin hand held a cane;
With silvery locks blown far behind,
    He hurried through the lane,
Some straggling listener to find,
    And seldom sought in vain.

For often, in the dusty street,
    Men paused from work to hear
The echoes of the hills repeat
    The shrill voice of the seer;
And boys forgot each playful feat,
    And idly clustered near.

The baby left its mother's arm
    To hear the old man sing;
And cream-white fingers, plump and warm,
    Around his lips would ring,
To pluck the song's mysterious charm, —
    The winsome, witless thing!

And little girls, upon a bank
  Of blossoms red and white,
Pausing amid some pretty prank,
  Their eyes with fun still bright,
Listened, while timidly they shrank;
  It was a pleasant sight:

For he was harmless in his mood,
  And told, with cheerful tone,
True stories of the wise and good,
  To Hebrew ages known: —
In ways we little understood,
  His seeds of truth were sown.

And so he wandered east and west,
  And up and down the land;
We wondered if, at night, his rest
  Were on the hard, bare sand;
He surely had one sheltering nest, —
  The hollow of God's hand.

It seemed to us he could not die,
    Nor yet with years grow old.
His home was somewhere in the sky,
    For aught we could have told;
And had he, wingless, tried to fly,
    Who would have thought him bold?

Thou weird apostle of the Past,
    Among the shoots of May
Was thy unsifted seed-grain cast;
    And with her blossoms gay,
The wayside word has bloomed at last,
    More beautiful than they.

Dead? In thy right mind thou dost sit
    Upon Life's farther shore,
Bathed in the Light that men of wit
    With dazed eyes shrink before;
While, on a pauper's grave is·writ,
    " Here slumbers Larkin Moore."

WHAT THE TRAIN RAN OVER.

WHEN the train came shrieking down,
   Did you see what it ran over?
I saw heads of golden brown,
   Little plump hands filled with clover.
Yes, I saw them, boys and girls,
   With no look or thought of flitting,
Not a tremble in their curls; —
   Where the track runs they were sitting.

From the windows of the train
   I could see what they were doing:
I could see their faces, plain;
   Some with dreamy eyes pursuing

Flight of passing cloud or bird;
    Others childish ditties flinging
On the air, — I almost heard
    What the song was they were singing.

They were well-known faces, too;
    Do you marvel that I shiver
As I picture them to you
    Playing there beside the river?
With them I myself have played
    On that very spot. I wonder
Why I never was afraid
    Of the coming railway-thunder.

Little, sunburnt, barefoot boys
    In the shallow water wading,
Sea-birds scattering with your noise,
    Ragged hats your rogue-looks shading,
Will your sparkling eyes upon
    Yonder waves again flash never?

WHAT THE TRAIN RAN OVER.

Is your heartsome laughter gone
   From this tired old world forever?

Dimpled Ruth, with brow of snow, —
   Never thought I to outlive her,
While we watched the white boats go
   Up and down the small tide-river,
Past dark steeps of juniper,
   Ever widening, ever flowing
To the sea; I mourn for her,
   Gone so far beyond my knowing!

Well, the cruel train rolls on.
   What! your eyes with tears are filling
For my pretty playmates gone?
   Child, I am to blame for chilling
All your warm young fancies so:
   There are real troubles, plenty.
They lived — forty years ago;
   And the road has run here twenty.

And those children, — I was one, —
   Busy men and women, wander
Under life's midsummer sun.
   One or two have gone home yonder
Out of sight. But still I see
   Golden heads amid the clover
On the railway-track ; to me
   This is what the train runs over.

STARLIGHT.

MOTHER, see! the stars are out,
Twinkling all the sky about;
Faster, faster, one by one,
From behind the clouds they run.
Are they hurrying forth to see
Children watching them like me?

"Oft I wonder, mother dear,
Why so many stars appear
Through the darkness every night,
With their little speck of light:
Hardly can a ray so small
Brighten up the world at all."

"Ah, you know not, little one,
Every dim star is a sun
To some planet-circle fair,
In its far-off home of air.
Rays that here so faint you call,
There in radiant sunshine fall.

"I have sometimes wondered, too,
(Scarcely wiser, dear, than you,)
Why unnumbered souls had birth
On this wide expanse of earth;
Wondered where the need was shown
For so many lives unknown.

"He who calls the stars by name,
At his mighty word they came
Out of heaven's deep light, to bless
Life's remotest wilderness.
Every soul may be a sun, —
You and I, too, little one!"

IF I WERE A SUNBEAM.

IF I were a sunbeam,
   I know what I'd do;
I would seek white lilies
   Rainy woodlands through.
I would steal among them,
   Softest light I'd shed,
Until every lily
   Raised its drooping head.

"If I were a sunbeam,
   I know where I'd go;
Into lowliest hovels,
   Dark with want and woe:

Till sad hearts looked upward,
 I would shine and shine;
Then they 'd think of heaven,
 Their sweet home and mine."

Art thou not a sunbeam,
 Child, whose life is glad
With an inner radiance
 Sunshine never had?
O, as God hath blessed thee,
 Scatter rays divine!
For there is no sunbeam
 But must die or shine.

BRING BACK MY FLOWERS.

A CHILD beside a rivulet
    With half-blown flowers
      Sat garlanded:
She scattered them, with dew-drops wet,
    While noiseless hours
      Unnoticed sped.

She threw them on the sparkling stream, —
    Her blossoms bright, —
      Till all were gone.
She saw her rosebuds' eddying gleam,
    As out of sight
      They drifted on.

"Bring back my flowers!" aloud she cried.
    With toss of spray
        The idle wave
Sent mocking echoes to her side,
    But bore away
        The gift she gave.

O little child beside life's stream,
    Love garlands you
        With moments bright:
The days are wasting while you dream:
    Their bloom and dew
        Fade out of sight.

Let gentle thoughts and gentler deeds
    With fragrance rare
        Fill all your hours!
For Time glides on, and never heeds
    Your weeping prayer,
        "Bring back my flowers!"

SNOW-SONG.

HEAR a bird chirp in the sun;
   He flutters and hops to and fro;
   His tiny light tracks, one by one,
   He prints on the new-fallen snow.
Little bird, sing!
Sun, give his wing
A flicker of gold as you go!
Make a smooth path for him, Snow!

I see a child out there at play;
   His footfall is light on the snow;

His curls catch a swift golden ray
   Of the sun, while the merry winds blow.
      Little child, run!
      Shine on him, Sun!
Blow him fair weather, Wind, blow!
Make a white path for him, Snow!

The little bird's home is the sky,
   Or the ground, or a nest in the tree.
The little child some day will fly
   From his doorstep, new regions to see.
      Bird-like and free
      May his sunny flight be!
And wherever on earth he may go,
May his footsteps be whiter than snow!

NEW-YEAR'S WISHES.

NEW-YEAR'S morning softly broke
　　As a little girl awoke,
And, half rising in her bed,
To her drowsy sister said:
"Waken, Annie! Where's the bird?
Where's the singing that I heard?
Birds and birds went to and fro,
Thick and white as flakes of snow,

Singing sweetly as they flew;
Never came such music through
Thrush's beak or linnet's throat.
How I wished that I could float
In the air, and sing so, too!
Listen, Annie! one bird flew
In here, fluttering down to you.
How he came I could not learn;
But the white tips of the fern
Jack Frost painted on the pane
Waved in and waved out again,
As that white bird came and went.
O, I wonder what it meant!
Warm, soft wings and bubbling song;
Where, where could those birds belong,
Making all the frosty sky
Tingle, ring, as they went by?"

Annie murmured: "Strange, you seem
Not to know it was a dream."

"O, but, Annie! wake and hear!
Happy New Year to you, dear!
Wake up! It is New-Year's day!
On your pillow there's a ray
Of the golden morning sun."

Then a low voice: "Little one,
Of the birds I heard you tell,
And I know their meaning well.
New-Year's wishes, happy words,
Were the dear white singing-birds
Thronging in the snowy air.
Think how sweet, if everywhere,
When a loving word were said,
Birds went warbling overhead!
And, perhaps, to ear and eye
Of the watchers in the sky
So it is; with each kind thought
Song and flash of wing is brought
To our world from gardens bright,

Where no winter is, nor night.
Call your birds the Christ-child's doves;
For the music that he loves
Is the carol, 'Peace! Good-will!'
Echoing from his birthday still;
And the birthday of the year
Brings again the Christ-child here."

"Then the bird on Annie's head
Was the New-Year's wish I said,
Mother darling? This does seem
Something better than a dream."

ON THE STAIRWAY.

THE little children on the stairway
    Cased in a slippery glare of sleet,
By post and railing vainly clamber;
    Slight hold is there for baby-feet.
High in the cold air swings the school-bell;
    "Come up! come up!" its clang commands;
A quick thought flies from lips to fingers, —
    "'T is easier, taking hold of hands."

Now laughter lights their rosy faces;
    Stout arms the faltering strugglers lift;
Now all at last have won the threshold,
    And out of sight within they drift,

Flinging back bloom upon the snow-wreaths;
   The blank, white world reflects their smile :
Their word has cleared for us a pathway,
   Though Alps of ice the highroad pile.

We all are children on a stairway,
   Weary of vain attempts to climb,
Or, strong ourselves, forgetting others;
   While silver peals of duty chime
High in the beckoning heaven above us;
   And, welcome we or dread the call,
Upon the steps we may not linger, —
   Ascend we must, slide back, or fall.

Whose is the fault if this one stumbles,
   If that laments a hopeless bruise,
Or if another sits despairing?
   Yours, — mine, — who timely aid refuse.
Small honor, to go up unhindered
   While a tired brother by us stands.

The little children, they shall teach us
"'T is easier, taking hold of hands."

Still up and down on Virtue's ladder
　Unnumbered beings come and go,
With faces turned to nether darkness,
　Or sunned with a celestial glow.
The truants out of Duty's heaven,
　The white and dazzling seraph-bands,
Are brethren still; and, struggling upward,
　"T is easier, taking hold of hands."

THE LITTLE TAMBOURINE-GIRL.

I REMEMBER a dear little girl
    Whose feet kept time to a tambourine,
The sunless walls of the street between.
    Her hair had a breezy curl,
    Her brown eye was merry and wild, —
        That gay little child
    Who danced up and down
The brick-red walks of the tiresome town.

    I watched her day after day;
And I wished I could have her for my own,
To dance in the fields, among daisies blown,
    With the wind in her hair at play,
    And her heart as light as a breeze,

Swaying under the trees
Unto bird-notes, swung
Through the blossomed boughs that above her hung.

That little motherless maid!
(No mother would let her darling go
Through the wicked streets of the city so,)
I know not where she has strayed;
But her memory shadows my dreams,
And her brown eye gleams
Upon me in reproof
That I hold 'so long from her fate aloof.

Every sweet little girl I see
Growing up like a rose at a cottage-door,
Or softly at play on the forest floor,
Or under the orchard tree,
Seems to murmur in my ear,
So sadly, so clear:
"Alas! we miss a mate!
For the dear little dancing girl we wait."

Yet I knew not her home or name;
And one and another passed her by, —
Nobler and richer women than I. —
   To whom belongs the blame
    When a blossom of snow and fire
     Trodden down in the mire
    Of the city is seen?
Ah me! for my child with the tambourine!

AT NIGHTFALL.

WHAT is it that we children feel,
  When by our little beds we kneel
And speak to Some One out of sight
Above the heavens so high, so bright?
It scarce is wonder, scarce is fear,
That thrills our thought of Some One near.

We say "Our Father!" when we wake.
What, with the sunrise, seems to break
Through every flower, like a surprise,
As if a thousand loving eyes
Looked out from sunbeams, buds, and dew,
And said, "He is our Father, too!"

We little children stand and gaze
At the white evening star, whose rays
Beam down upon us, like an eye
Forever open in the sky,
Through the strange twilight asking this
Of one another: "Is it His?"

We little children find it sweet
To cling about His unseen feet,
When in some troubled dream we moan,
And wake to find ourselves alone;
So sweet — that we are in His care
Who sees us, loves us everywhere!

Who is He? That we cannot say.
He is. And by his side to stay,
To love Him in the flowers and birds,
In dear home-faces, tender words,
In all things beautiful and true, —
No more than this we ask to do.

AT NIGHTFALL.

Our Father, every day more dear
It seems to live, with Thee so near.
Thou carest for even the smallest star,
And safe within thy heart we are.
If left alone on earth are we,
We are not orphans! we have Thee!

CHRISTMAS GREEN.

BRING in the trailing forest-moss;
   Bring cedar, fir, and pine;
And green festoon, and wreath, and cross,
   Around the windows twine!

Against the whiteness of the wall
   Be living verdure seen,
Sweet summer memories to recall,
   And keep your Christmas green.

CHRISTMAS GREEN.

It is His dear memorial-day,
  Who broke earth's frozen sleep,
And who for her hope's gladdening ray
  Forever bright will keep.

He gives all loveliness that grows:
  The strong and graceful trees,
The winter moss, the fresh June-rose,
  The dear Lord saves us these,

Who saves us from the piteous wreck
  Of souls adrift in sin.
So not alone the churches deck,
  But peaceful homes within, —

Made peaceful by His constant love, —
  Let thoughts of Him abide;
To find us our lost home above,
  He homeless lived and died.

And where would be the heart to smile,
    Where any cheer or mirth,
If from its sin-blot, black and vile,
    He could not cleanse the earth?

Not for a superstition's sake,
    Borne down from ages dead,
We love to see this morning break
    In sunshine overhead;

Not as a day of heedless mirth,
    A feast-day rude and wild,
We hail its dawn, — but for the birth
    Of the world's dearest Child,

We keep the bright home-festival;
    And, with a childlike cheer,
His angel-ushered birthday call
    The merriest of the year.

CHRISTMAS GREEN.

Yes, — merry Christmas let it
    be !
A day to love and give !
Since every soul's best gift is
    He
  Who came that we might
    live ;

And all things beautiful are
    his,
  And his he maketh ours ;
So bring each bud that burst-
    ing is,
  All Christmas-blooming flow-
    ers ;

All blossoms that in windows
    shine,
  With leaves to light un-
    furled, —

In memory of that Flower Divine
　Whose fragrance fills the world!

Be all old customs honored so,
　That good to others mean!
Bring cross and garland from the snow,
　And keep your Christmas green!

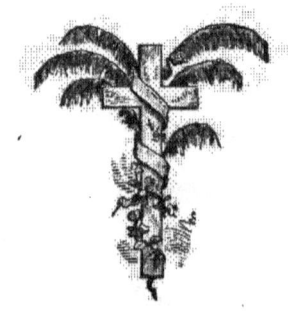

MY CHILDREN.

THEY are a beauteous family,
    Sweet sisters and brave brothers;
Too many for one house, you see,
And so I have to let them be
    In care of other mothers.

They go by other names than mine;
    But names have little meaning:
They know me by some secret sign;
And roseleaf cheeks and fingers fine
    Towards me come clinging, leaning.

None of them all I claim alone;
    With other hearts I share them:
But this the common lot is known:

All mothers, when their babes are grown,
    To the wide world must spare them.

My loveliest children never go
    Out of my happy dwelling;
No mortal parentage they know,
Though on the walls "Correggio"
    And "Raphael" you are spelling.

Not quite so dear as flesh and blood,
    They are to me most real:
In them I see heaven's childhood bud;
These little human stars that stud
    The skies of the Ideal.

That land of glorious mystery
    Whither we all are wending,
A lonely sort of heaven will be,
If there no baby-family
    Awaits my love and tending.

MY CHILDREN.

Windows of mansions in the skies
    Must glow with infant faces,
Or somewhere else is Paradise:
The lovely laughter of their eyes
    Lights up all heavenly places.

My darlings! by my mother-heart
    I have found, I shall find them.
Though some from me are worlds apart,
And, thinking of them, tears will start
    Into my eyes, and blind them.

O little ones whom I have found
    Among earth's green paths playing,
Though listening far behind, around,
They bring me still the sweetest sound, —
    Words I have heard you saying.

O little ones whom I shall see
    On floors of golden glory,
I guess how fair your looks will be,

When your sweet voices lisp to me
    Your beautiful new story.

It was a little Child who swung
    Wide back that City's portal
Where hearts remain forever young;
And, all things good and pure among,
    Shall childhood be immortal.

THE END.

www.ingramcontent.com/pod-product-compliance
Lightning Source LLC
Chambersburg PA
CBHW032225230426
43666CB00033B/1598